Praise for Un/Broken

'Kate Jenkinson talks about her life
frankness, an easy humour, and a
loved ones captured in these page
childhood, finding courage through friendships, motherhood,
menopause, and the workplace, with a wry glare at those who
claim diversity without actually taking the time to understand
people.
Inherently personal and political, Un/Broken is a headfirst tackling
of the social model of disability and our understanding of
neurodivergence in the workplace, in our schools, in our lives, but
Kate's steady hand doesn't let us stray to a sad place. The book
emulates Kate's own presence in the literary community, as a
guiding light trying to ease the passage for other neurodivergent
people trying to find their way. With resilience ringing like a bell
through every poem we are left, instead, celebrating all the hope
found within.' – **Kathryn O'Driscoll**

'From heart-break to heart-make, Kate has perfectly encapsulated
the tonality of her journey within this collection. Through her own
experiences, Kate holds up a mirror to the reader, helping them
see themselves in her words. She is a true lyricist, and a must-
have representative for the neurodiverse community.' – **Charlotte
Faulconbridge**

'A personal, and ultimately hopeful, collection of poetry, that
grapples with family, friendship, ageing and productivity through
the lens of increasing self-awareness of the author's own
neurodivergence. By turns funny, poignant and life-affirming.' –
Leanne Moden

Un/Broken

by
Kate Jenkinson

Un/Broken – Kate Jenkinson

First published 2024 by Poetic Edge Publishers
Tunstall, Stoke-on-Trent, UK

ISBN 978-1-917408-00-4

Edited by Ashley Edge

Cover design by G Sabini-Roberts
Cover art by G Sabini-Roberts
Typeset by Ashley Edge

Printed and bound by Amazon KDP

A catalogue for this book is available from the British Library.

For
Shaun, James and Maria

Introduction

Born into the world vulnerable, yet fully unknown to ourselves, we are all on the journey of self-discovery.

My first collection of poetry delves into this universal truth and discovers the uniqueness that is there for each of us to find, should we choose to seek it. From not knowing, a visceral yearning to know, finally to acceptance, we come full circle through mind, body and soul as poetry speaks the truth I cannot visualise as images in my mind.

To take this journey I had to listen, acutely, to the sense we develop first in the womb: hearing. Everything that grows starts in the dark, I've been listening intently to the sound of my soul speaking for the last 8 years. This coincided with poetry coming back into my life. I was seeking an ease and restfulness I'd never felt.

This collection begins with the angry spirit endeavouring to be heard, having a voice, but it not being the right one; making an impact but not with the right executive presence. It tracks the deep curiosity, the compelling yearning I have always had, to understand why I wasn't fitting in and how to change that.

Many neurodivergent folks feel broken, not enough, or too much in this world. Without my friends I wouldn't have understood how to unbreak myself. Through truly connecting with my spirit, I have found the words that reconcile all my disparate parts; all the hats I wear are now united in this collection of poetry and I hope through me finding my truth you have a glimpse of your own.

And as we are all born naked and vulnerable into this world, so I hope to leave it: with no regrets…

Contents

Feelings flow freely,
experience grows value;
everyone prospers.

NeuroDelusion

Belonging is perceived
through embodied being.
If my needs aren't believed
then inclusion is a delusion.

The writing is on the wall.

Neuroinclusion is bringing
my whole self to work.
If I must ignore a part of me
because you do – know that I can't.

The writing is on the wall.

The additional cognitive load
will cause an explosion
or implosion, result
in my exclusion.

The writing was on the wall.

This burnout wasn't in my control.
It's environmental: A denial
of the fundamental human right
not to be exposed to discrimination.

The writing was on the wall.

Even if it's invisible to you,
ignorance is no defence;
your duty of care is all.
Hear my voice:

The writing was on the wall.

When All Else Fails

Your career is a solo trip,
your life cannot be lived by others.

Remember: When you need advice
you have your head, your heart,
your gut and your soul to ask.

And when there's nothing in reply
remember your lungs,
your breath, will get you by.

Cookie Cutter Creativity

Despite the fact that children
are not made of clay,
we're going to judge their talents
                              in a cookie cutter way.

We decide the rules of play –
the As, the Bs, the Cs, the Ds –
and we'll label everything they say
so, they will fail to succeed. Unless
they tick our box
                              in a cookie cutter way.

We've made it very clear,
the answer must be ours.
Their originality and lateral thinking
are a waste of their thinking powers.

They must learn to curb creative thought
and learn everything by rote.
So, no matter if they're bored,
unless it ticks our box,
their thinking is clearly flawed.

So, despite the fact that children
are not made of clay,
we're going to judge their talents
                              in a cookie cutter way.

So, it really is annoying
when they interpret someone's poem
with a phrase or form that does not conform,
because it means I cannot tick the box that says
they understand how to behave
                              in a cookie cutter way.

And it's even more frustrating
when their talent shines all day,
but they won't let me catch it and control it.
Because they are not made of clay,
and it's so much easier to compare them
                              in a cookie cutter way.

So, now they are all labelled wrong
and we're both disturbed by this.
But rather than it be our problem,
it's clearly *they* who've got it wrong.

So, please change your personalities, children,
to reflect our world view.
Then we can tick our little box
which dispenses with the problem
that is
                              you.

And yet, despite the fact that people
are not made of clay,
organisations persist their measuring
                              in a cookie cutter way.

Our collective creativity
will be performance managed away
so the human work experience
is only ever shades of beige.

And despite the fact
                                that not one of us
is made of clay,
they will only ever recognise you
                                      in a cookie cutter way.

Their expectations are impossible
and distribution's normal.
The categories are now only three –
does not meet, meets, exceeds –
and the conversations are all formal.

I will not be fired in someone else's kiln.
I am not glazed to meet the norms.
I do not aspire to be plastic clay.
So, I'm making creativity my enterprise
and tossing
                                  that cookie cutter away.

All My First Jobs

A volunteer at the RSPCA
unpaid
mostly shovelling shit
and marvelling at the colours

A volunteer at The Geology Museum
unpaid
mostly unpacking crumbling
rocks in rotting boxes

A locker room assistant
at an unheated outdoor pool
mostly paid
for shivering whilst reading

A box office assistant
at The Palace Theatre
mostly paid
for stuffing envelopes

An evening receptionist
for adult evening classes
mostly paid
for smiling sweetly

A practical assistant
for degree students
mostly paid
for refocussing microscopes

A staff development administrator
for a local college
mostly paid
for hacking the computer

And then HR Adviser
for a corporate
mostly paid
as a messenger to shoot
between Unions and Management

Finding a knack for listening
to the underlying needs of people
Finding the beauty in business
and meaning in the mundane

Undiagnosed
(First published in 'Poetry For All' anthology 2023)

An abundance of areas
Demanding my attention
How can I prioritise them
Don't tell me to 'just focus'

Are you aware of your bias
Describing me as lazy
However hard I work it just
Doesn't ever seem to be enough

And I try to imagine every sleight
Disaster scenario planning as I go
Hoping I get it right this time
Despite your constant criticism

And sometimes you are kind
Deciding to ask me what I need
How can I say what it is when I
Don't even know myself?

Resignation

…..Really??!!!
begins your email
with your opinion black on white – piercing
        my open heart
with your disrespectful frustration
spiked with managerial spite

I'm smited

by a claw-headed hammer
hitting unseen nails – problems
of your making in my mind

…..Really??!!!
I'm here, again, where
one person's view trumps all others
dialogue dissolves unheard
like the ibuprofen I take
for another migraine headache

a pounding headache
from overthinking how
to meet expectations unspoken
respond to feedback ungiven
react to criticism scattered liberally
and
        STILL
                BE
    ME

imperceptibly the emails change
and I think 'now we're collaborating!'
'now we're getting on!'
not realising the turn
in phrase was you withdrawing
your support
what I mistook for respect
was the imminent threat
of another
        bitter
          ending

when the day arrived
and I was told to stop

I was angry with relief
exhausted from trying
close to my third collapse
and too worn out for crying
from my stress-related efforts
to adapt to you
when you never seemed
to want to work with me

and again I wonder
how I got hooked two years ago
by the shiny strapline
that diversity fits in
and everyone belongs
I swallowed that worm
          WHOLE

now I'm eviscerated
and that's what happens
at the end – the toxic cultures
poison us
      leave us
           with hearts
  beating
arrhythmically

never forget
most workplaces
are responsibility traps
hidden behind counterfeit
emotions and smiling human
faces

Busyness

is seductive
sucks us into rumination
despite our determination
to be mindful

Busyness

is addictive
makes us feel productive
feeds our activity
with fresh dopamine hits
fills our thinking space
as we seek another fix
this always-on management
creates an ecosystem
of never getting
the important work done
constantly forgetting

Busyness

kills our compassion
burns out inspiration
smokes our eyes
strokes our egos
sucks our souls dry

Workplace Rubric

What will it take to break the bias?
How can we make sense within this chaos?

How many rules and expectations
of our 21st century workplace
do we need to
- challenge
- change
- replace?

How much
- educational
- institutional
- emotional

conditioning do we need to erase?

Are one woman's words enough?
Why is equality still a gendered thing?
The common denominator
is surely our   **humanity.**

That's the level we need to aspire to.
That's the central purpose
our policies should seek to enshrine.

Not some category that can be ticked.
We need to kick the numbers
out (as a measure of success)
and introduce another test of fairness.

We need more recognition. Less reward.
More intelligence in our board rooms.
The processes we routinely use
are not fit for human empowerment.
They simply make the mechanics
of our balance sheets predictable.
We need to lose our tried and tested go-to's:

Drop	the individualistic performance related pay
Drop	the retention bonuses to make arrogant people stay
Swap	the negotiations that favour the traditional characteristics of ego-centred leadership
Drop	the power-play and politics
Drop	the aggressive tactics used to put those down who lift others up

What will it take to break the bias?
Equality requires a harmony.

It will take a chorus
of all of us
working together.

Centred

My	life	now balanced
between Mother and	wife	
forever on the	wire	I tightrope dance in clothes
I never chose, but	wore	
because the	work	demanded it!
Until I	wore	my heart on my sleeve.
My choice is to	wire	myself more courageously.
Not only	wife	and Mother.
I'm married to the	life	I love.

Everything that grows
starts in the dark.

Work Life Balance

I had a Father
who went to work
and it was his life

I had a Mother
who had a life
and it was her work

I don't remember my Father
I shall never forget my Mother

Love Equals
(after 'A Portable Paradise' by Roger Robinson)

And when you sat me,
trembling, on your knee
unable to speak my terror,
through sobs, of another maths
lesson I couldn't bear

you took me home.
All day I played shop;
selling ice cream cones
of cotton wool, gaining
confidence to show up
at school again.

In my pocket, a rough,
blue, rubbed-round
eraser, so I could remember
that I am not defined
by my long division mistakes.

Yorkshire Puddings

'For what we are about to receive,
may the Lord make us truly thankful'

And in the blue corner
we have Kate, always late, covered in mud,
hands unclean and hair a mess,
never wearing her Sunday best.

I wash my hands, comb out my tangles,
sit up nicely, close my eyes,
palms together in prayer whilst Nana
says grace as menacingly as the Haka.

In the red corner
we have a Roast Lamb dinner, plated like
a Giant Haystack, waiting for the DING DING
of the bell. The ref shouts *'let's wrestle!'*

Round 1! I grab my fork and pin the sprouts
into submission, smash potato into cabbage,
toss the lamb with mint sauce and pinch my nose
as everything goes down in one.

Round 2! Extra points for innovation, smothering
the carrots with gravy to disguise their unsavoury
flavours and trying to hide the gristle under my knife.
I avoid the choking fat for my life.

Round 3! Penalty points awarded:
The meat has been discovered and there will
be no pudding unless my plate is empty.

On the canvas now. Shoulders heaving
as I'm being counted out 6   7   8

I grab the jug, take a massive slug of water,
liquefy the slimy strands and swallow them whole.
This reversal brings a cheer from my sister.

Round 4! Tarty gooseberry grapples
the crumble, overwhelming my taste buds
in a headlock of sweet and sour. I twist my face,
twist in my seat, triumphantly ask

'Please may I leave the table?'

Sibling Symmetry

I was the cowboy
to your damsel in distress
I wore the gun holster
You wore the dress

I was the rescuer
when your bullies descended
I wore the bruises
You were defended

I was the bride
and penniless
You made me proud
and a wedding dress

I was the bread winner
The toil: relentless
You rescued my feelings
My gratitude: endless

Short Straws

I'll huff and I'll puff and I'll blow your house in!

Sometimes luck draws
you the short straw
and that's when it's all to play for!

When life kicks you to your knees
it would be easy to stay down
and grieve the chances you lost
from your lot in life.

But that is not what has been my way.

Planned second child
then homeless at one;
the protector, our father, what a brick!
Left for the love of another one –
my Mum's best friend.

No wonder Mum suffered
as her marriage collapsed.
Clutching at straws in the end;
her crashing depression
nearly crushed my elder sister and me,
as we fought to be seen
in the rubble and heartbreak.
Ages just 1 and 3.

A knock on the door saved us all
as Mum felt obliged to answer this call.
Removing her head from the jaws
of suicide, our gas oven, the only possession
surviving because everything else
had been sold. Our futures on hold
then slowly imploding.

Mum traumatised, was hospitalised
as all our straws blew away in the storms.
We plunged into a poverty of nothingness.
No mother, no father, no home, no money, no voice.
When you are small you have no choice
but to make good with the hand you are dealt.

And you can't make bricks without straw.

From emptiness our tiny family rebuilt.
My Grandpa as guarantor secured us a house
and with nothing but love for us
my Mum made a home. Working shifts
as a cleaner, shop assistant, caregiver,
she did whatever she could
to afford the food on our knees.

And there were days she didn't eat
'cos the money couldn't stretch that far.
She struggled with eating
and how people perceived her:
A young mother alone
raising two small daughters.
The stigma was palpable.

Single mothers are to blame after all
and that shame sticks.

The burden of guilt they stacked
on our 'broken home' hit us
repeatedly like a tonne of bricks.
I wanted none of it.

When our dog ran away
and my Grandpa died –
that was my final straw.
I wanted to run far, far away
and be lost forever;
nowhere felt safe
with the wolf
scratching at the door.

Sometimes luck draws
you the short straw
but I'm stubbornly strong
because I struggled so young
and because my Mum didn't quit.

I've grown up learning:
A loving home is assured
when built from shit and sticks,
a Mother's grit and lots and lots of short straws,

equally as well as from bricks.

If my scars could talk
(Earlier version published in 'EyeFlash' Magazine)

If the scar on my left
hand could speak
it would shout:
'Look before you reach!'

The scar on the knuckle
of my left foot would
have a few more words to say:
'Don't cycle so fast,
especially downhill
at speed; don't
close your eyes,
you'll crash
into trees!'

The scar on my abdomen
would look
at your broad
shoulders and whisper:
'Thank you'.

Cake

You
are the icing
on the cake that you baked
the fondant smile that you make, with
your hands, is mine, as I watch you: the cake we
baked 22 years ago, when you were the little bun in my oven.

Absence

If I said
I love you

the words
would only be skin deep

when it's with my heart's beat
I love you
           so deep
                deep
                    deep

I love you
        I can't
              sleep
                  without
something
to remind me of you.

Missing in Action

where do all my teaspoons go
I scratch my head, jangle
the survivors in their tray

wonder if the escapees swam
to safety with the dregs
of last night's take-away

slipped between the dinner plates
rejoiced in the sprinkling of hot
showers, grinning upside down

at each other as they fled
gliding, quicksilver
shimmering in the moonlight

Moving On

the smooth handled brush
warms to my touch

the swish and the swirl
as we gather the dust
remnants of meals
vegetable peelings
my unwanted feelings

the sweep and the swash
as I pile them together
the bits and the bobs
satisfying jobs
a heap of what was

swallowed by the dustpan
swiftly brushed off

Through you seeing me
for the best I can be,
my potential is realised

A Pocket in Time

Our Friendship was a pocket in time from age 9 to 16. My pockets were deep and unfillable, yours were deep and full of holes. We needed the same things, love and belonging; we filled each other's needs. It was a potent, imperfect match. You poured out passion, emotion and opinion and I was full. My self-esteem intact ONLY when I was with you, and I was ALWAYS with you. Whereas my love fell constantly through the holes of your self-doubt, a persistent gentle shower heading always to the drain. I wanted to save you! Rescue you! I sewed up all the holes in your pockets. I mended your hurt, but your pain became trapped, and it was never released. As you grew you found friends who soothed and admired you in different ways, filling other needs that I couldn't. And I did the same. Why it was I who felt betrayed, I don't know. Neither of us betrayed the other.

That crime was committed by our Fathers long ago.

Years of neglect for me, and your innocence was stripped clean away before you could choose your fate. Our Mothers had to live with the consequences – their choices became our lives. We were close, inextricably connected. A self-fulfilling pocket in time, together we made sense of this wilderness. Rendezvous at 10.30pm, bring significant items preserved in a plastic bag: a photo of us, a Lego figurine, 14½p; a scribbled note: clutched in my pocket. The place: the corner oak tree with its gnarled bark; the one that concealed notes under its skin and watched us play frisbee and rounders by day. My torch lit the tarmac, broken glass glinting back the dangers of night. Our 11-year-old memories buried under the Town Fields turf. Our secret: delicious; savoured each night, pieces of us that no one could touch. Safe. Then forgotten.

Our paths diverged. We lived separate adult lives, compartmentalised to keep us safe.

I heard you died by suicide.

I remember our shared, buried memories and wish for life's significance to be purely: Lego, pennies and a photo of you and me. I put down my pen, fold this note, clutch it in my pocket.

Bury it under the corner oak tree.

Double-Dutch

our peers made it clear
              we didn't belong
the words that we used
              were too long
the ways that we dressed
              were fashionless
the clothes we were given
              were plain wrong
the phrases we made up
              were pretentious
and contentiously
              we didn't exchange this
for acceptable phrases
              to say what we meant
we discovered more
              incongruent ways
to be present
              with no malicious intent
except to honour ourselves
              and our difference
we spoke Double-Dutch
              they didn't understand much
nattering about nonsense
              as if it mattered
making new nothingness
              to soothe the gaping wounds

    of bullying and indifference

Regret

I wonder why I have no friends
I wish I had stayed in touch
I wish you were still here
I wonder at all the letters I never sent
SOS messages bobbing lost at sea
I think of all the time I wasted

I think of all the love I wasted
There are many different kinds of friend
My heart is driftwood in the sea
We cannot hug if we fear to touch
I miss you now you are absent
Your voice is the one thing I long to hear

Your absence casts a shadow here
I think of all the joy I wasted
Your flowers pressed have no scent
Solitude can sometimes be a friend
Your old letters smell of your touch
I may long for you but will never see

As I often look wistfully out to sea
It's when I notice most, you are not here
Our hands in each other's, warmth in touch
Our friendship was never wasted
I didn't know what made you a special friend
I never thought beyond the present

I wish your goodbyes were never sent
Broken apart by things I couldn't see
I have no one else to call my friend
Recalling conversations I no longer hear
I think of all the hope I wasted
I miss your closeness and your touch

Time twists away as I strain to touch
Your memories, their melancholy scent
Reminds me of the life I've wasted
Watching footprints washed away by sea
Leaving me stranded always alone, here
When all I wanted was you: my friend

Could I have stayed in touch? I was no friend
to you, I see now how much effort you wasted
trying to be present for me, to be here, to be loved.

Where does weird fit?

it doesn't does it?
like soft clay I was fired
my heart barb-wired

as you drop me
I don't bounce, I shatter
I was never broken before
but now I am

if I upset you
would you let me know
or have me forget
that we were friends?

if I upset you
would you share
how that was so
so we can make amends?

if not
my heart can't take
another fracture / break
respect my boundaries
don't be too friendly

46

Awakening

My soul aches
for a friend who takes
my mistakes and makes
them learning, who turns
the burning shame I feel;
reframes it, renames it:
Love.

I didn't trust myself. But
feeling this raw – exposed –
makes me wonder what
clothed me before. I won't
be reaching for that
anymore.

I lay me bare before you.
There is no fight, flight, freeze
or fawn, just the naked truth;
a vulnerable connection.
I trust you like a newborn.
I'm home.

Un/Broken

A million words shared
bound us
A few ill-chosen words
broke us apart

But a friendship as precious
as ours is a kintsugi vase

All the more special
for the careful
reconstruction
and the golden glue
of forgiveness

that binds and blunts
the sharpest shards

Poetry Pen Pals
(after "You're Like" by Sylvia Plath)

You are the horse running, muscles rippling
I am the thudding of hooves on well-trod turf

Your movement, like gold dust in sunbeams
I am the wooden curtain rings sliding on the pole

You are the gently wafting curtain at the open window
I am the young boy's whistle in the street below

You are the milk van floating on the road
I am the rattle-clink of empty, crated bottles

You are the vast beauty of the arched rainbow
I am the hushed breath of awe from weary workers

You are the Kaleidoscope mirrors
                    with colours shifting constantly

I am the crunch–crack–turn
                    as the beads resist the twisting

Synergy

My smile
is a simile
for our friendship.

1
syllable
multiplied
to 3.

Your kindness
multiplies me.

Tapestry of Friendship

We untangle knots,
find each other at the end of blind alleys;
turn on the light of introspection
and guide each other
to new pathways.

We notice all the heaviness
weighting each other's words;
find the helium balloon of the moment
and tie the thoughts to each string
then let them do their thing.

We experience history and artefact,
drink tea and have a laugh.
We talk for hours and seconds pass.

We wonder at the craziness of it all,
drink more tea and quiet falls.
We sit in silence in each other's presence.

It feels like we've always been together,
but only in this moment finding
words that weave into blankets

that soothe the hurt. So, we keep
worrying at those knots together
with a gentle curiosity that inquiry

will find a way to free
the tangles that have defined you and me.
Until we made the strands of our identities

clear and bold and opinion free,
the loss and love and hollowness
was in every fibre of our beings.

Alone we had no way of seeing,
but the microscope of friendship does,
it shifts and sorts and heals us both.

There are as many
truths as minds to pursue it;
happiness ensues

Prioritise Your Addictions

Does my pain have a name? It does.
It's rejection   laced with blame.
I'm addicted to rejection like cocaine.

It's my line in the sand,
the back of my hand.
It's the place where my face doesn't fit.

I cover this shame, over and over with love.
Love for the beauty in others
and a niggling, wriggling, maggot-like belief,

I'm not worthy, buried in the heart of me.
But I'll fight for the right to be here
like I've fought all my life to be seen–believed–belong.

I'll over-share my vulnerability
attempting to make you care for me
and I'll expect you to do the same.

When I can categorise your pain,
I feel our connection is real.
I'm only curious because
your hurting makes me furious.

Who did this to you?

It would please me to release the locks
chaining your heart and pinning you down
like a butterfly preserved, reduced to mundanity.

And
your heart can't beat
                    if constrained by your fear
and
your love can't animate your dreams
                    if sleep doesn't keep you
                    immersed deep enough
and
your life can't be lived to the extremes of your joy
                    if your boundaries are smaller
                    than your happiness.

Does my pain have a name? It does.
It's perfection laced with shame.
I'm addicted to perfection like caffeine.

It's the migraine flashing
zig-zag lights in my brain.
It's the place where my face doesn't fit
                    and I don't see it.

I hide the shame with unconditional love.
Love for the wonder of others
and a niggling, wriggling maggot-like belief,

I'm never worthy, but I'll fight for the right
to be heard. Especially in places
where my face doesn't fit.

I fought all my life to be seen–believed–belong,
but I wonder if I don't hurt,
am I really here?

Resting Heartbeat

Dizziness
membrane
timpani
plays a
rhythm
for me
swoosh of
blood as
pressure
swoops low
cottoning
sound
a wave
a stress
drowning
beats from
my chest
stomach
replies
lurching
precar-
iously
I must
take this
precious
           precip-
                  itous
                        life more
                                 seri-
                                     ously

The GP Visit

Please come in.
Sit down.
Now, what's the matter?

Well, if I knew
do you think I'd be here to see you?
I'd have googled,
self-medicated
and sorted it out
but NO! I've had to come and admit
I'm failing at life.

i'm not sure

And that's just it:
I don't know!
It's not physical,
it's not anything I can pin down.
It's everything.
Diagnose that!

What symptoms
are you experiencing?

Well, everything's wrong,
nothing's right.
It's all black, not white;
every day grey, grey, grey
and I want the colour back
in my life.

i feel a bit down

**How long has this
been going on?**

> *If I knew I'd tell you.*
> *It's been going on forever.*
> *I've lost track of time,*
> *everything's merged into one.*
> *There's no joy, no sleep, no fun.*
> *No point*

a while

Fault Lines

Do you know where your edges are? I mean *do* you?
We are born without
edges.
It's the knocks we get,
            the scrapes we survive,
                        that create our edge.
Softness hardens to callous.

These callouses grow from pressing
our vulnerability into rock.
Again and again.

Some friction we choose,   some we couldn't possibly.

This pressure is where
            we could seek salvation
                        or release.
But we don't.

The traumas of teenage tremors
create seismic shifts in landscape;
shaping different paths.

            Fit in with parents   stand out from peers
            Fit in with peers   stand out from parents
            You cannot be both   we are told.
You must be
many personalities
other than your own   we are told.

            So we break.

Some break in the heart
     and build an armour of resistance.
Some break at the skin
     and the scars are visible.
Some break from reality
     because their dreams
          are more accessible.
Some break at the knees
     and others see the need
          to lift them.

Some break free from their body
     completely
and inhabit only their soul.

Life knocks us over
every
day.
No one bounces, not really.

We are brittle
in so many
different,
     shattering,
          ways.

Corporal Punishment

I pushed you hard: in sport,
in study, in life, at work.
I burnt you out three times at least.
I neglected, ignored, dehydrated
and undernourished you.

Dear Body,
          I am sorry I didn't learn
to love you more
when we were young.

I only noticed you in pain
or pleasure, never
in-between.

I rebelliously loved the features
others called out in playground names:
rubber lips, hairy legs, melancholy eyes.

I had to cover up
for shame of exposing thighs,
'above the knee', that others
should not see. Now I wish
I had been there for you, as you
have always been there for me.

Had I understood your needs
I may not have fallen so low.
Menopause feels like your revenge
as you demand attention
through every wayward regulation.

P.S.
      I will do my best to listen,
to understand the transformation
we are going through.

I must accept this for what it is:
a time to be wise, womanly, mature.
Where sleep, thoughts, thermoregulation,
nutrition, heart beats, beauty
are in transition.

Body,
      I will learn to love you more.

Manure

Inside my mind: A fertile void,
a humus soft womb that nurtures
my hurts, my hopes.

A blackboard yearning for an artist
with coloured chalks, the gift for writing
my thoughts aloud, drawing out my inspiration.

Sensing in the vulnerability
of the dark, incubating possibilities:
My lack of visual imagery releases me.

Black, where anything can germinate.
Black, where everything can shine.
Black: The beauty of my naked mind.

BitterSweet

(earlier version published in Petra Lens MSc thesis)

I sat beside my misery today
and listened to what she had to say.

She told me how she felt dejected,
ignored, cast out, always rejected.
She told me she was very sad,
that loss and heartache held her back;
that no one loved her and she was alone.

Her brown eyes filled with yearning sorrow.
She said she'd feel the same tomorrow.

I sat beside her in despair,
to see my own sad self-reflection there,
to know this truth is always inside me
and yet my heart keeps beating daily.
How could I guide her home safely?

I wanted, so much, to fix her hurting,
but knew no way to soothe her healing.

I gently warmed misery's hand in mine.
I said you'll understand in time,
that every person has a misery
struggling inside to be set free;
the constant conflict may disarm us.

Show us the path to inner peace.
It's not to ignore the bittersweet,
it's to give our misery a kind embrace,
to wipe the tears from her sweet face,
to say how much she means to you.

Her heartache makes us live more fully.
Hold her close, love her, unconditionally.

Not so sad to be beyond repair.
We are more than our scars and melancholy.
With acceptance, there's hope in the air
and a seat beside me, always,
for my misery.

Respair

I'd like to grasp the word Hope,
but the sharp possibilities
are razor blades incising my past
from my future, and Hope is the bridge

in-between

shaking and rattling, my nerves
slowly shattering and Hope,
although etched in my brain,
finds no fertile place

in my heart.

My hand extends
with my veins stretched blue,
exposed on my wrist. I shrug,
is it easier to end this

or exist with the pain?

Even Hope, with its hurting,
is worth me exerting myself
beyond the all-to-familiar fear.

I sense Hope is near.

I'd like to grasp the familiarity of Hope
for when Hope seemed to have
abandoned me, poetry rescued me;
ever there to find the words I couldn't hear.

Poetry reminded me that

Hope surges when pessimism pours
cold water on the fire of adventure.
Hope sizzles and spits her furious desire to be relit,

re lit.

Hope is the sunset on an imperfect day;
the sleeping rays, resting and re-energising,
darkness consuming all our fears
so, in the morning Hope dawns

and reappears.

She accompanies me in every new
and challenging experience,
her belief and sheer resilience
to cope with life's ups and downs.

I feel her gentle presence.

Hope holds my hand and whispers affirmations.
Her reassurance understands,
recharging my determination to survive,
inspiring my curiosity.

Hope keeps me alive.

'You *can* have it all!'

she said, proving it
by standing on the stage
proclaiming all her wins.
But is she like that in menopause
when her body is hormone-depleted,
her resilience defeated?

No one is there to pick her up
when she hears the words:
Your performance has dropped.

And I know.

I know it has.

I want to scream in despair
but I can't work out what to do
because no one in work
ever talks about this.

They share bravado, hubris, charisma,
as I drown in my own
hormonal drama.

Ageing

Who would be so foolish
as to compare
the youthful beauty
of the dawning sun

with the wisdom
of her face at dusk
when all her
radiance abounds?

Our sunset nights
are the most profound.
In your changing
face of beauty, trust.

Words create worlds,
what we focus on grows.

And Then There Were 4

As well as fight, flight, freeze –
                there's fawn!
I am the poetic definition of fawning –
                    a people pleaser,
not dissimilar to a Malteser!

I am a minstrel without the music;
heroic poetry set to rhythm.
Lyrical ideas ripple
out of me. Velvety smooth,
calmly cool.

I've a bounty
of love for the weary
drifters/travellers amongst us.

Mm the well-loved, much misunderstood
                    Malteser.
The cheeky teaser,
      topic/idea conceiver,
            moment seizer!

The nations favourite chocolate sweet.
One chomp, one suck and all
            shape
      is lost.
Sugar highs   crash
      into honeycomb crumbs.
All my boundaries collapsed, crossed.

Yes crossed.

I'm crossing the line
thinking I've finished a winner but
every time I'm fudging
the line of your trust.
This neurodiversity boundary
          between
you   and   me
makes careful communication
                    a must!

My right is your wrong,
              your right is a mystery to me.
I may be consumed/surrounded by your common sense
          but this is my originality.
I don't see the difference,
don't follow the inference,
never know the offence
          I've committed.

I'm not limited by
              'been there before's'.
I'm not contained by
              'this is the way it's always been done'.
If there's a new way to see it,
a better way to be it,
          I'm gonna follow that path.

If you judge a fish by its ability to climb trees
it will live its life believing it is stupid.
          I am that fish.

I'm a breath of fresh air, oh yes!
The wildcard in the recruitment slate;
the unconventional, innovative,
impossible to replicate,
revelling, rebellious
                    Kit-Kat Kate!

So, it's infuriating and anti-diversity
when you hire me for this
                    but expect me to fit in.
I refuse.
I'm remaining a fish.

Imagine the tree as/is the career ladder;
steps broken,
                    breaking.
        Gaps
where slats   should be.
That's how it's been for me.

A curly wurly career can be forced on you.
You get pushed off, time out, time after time.
Still, you try to climb back
        to where you were before.
It's snakes and ladders with loaded dice.
That's why Maltesers fawn;
that's why fish drown in air.

Vocabulary Test

like a child arriving too late for the last puppet show
or having a helium balloon accidentally let go
the ice cream melts all over clean clothes

my disappointment is stripped naked
humiliated, as separation anxiety overloads
and I scream into a sticky melting mess

it's high-functioning anxiety, dancing
with a highly sensitive personality
manifesting in its magnificent Sunday best

it's empathy on steroid-induced anxiety
every emotion amplified, nerve-endings
permanently fried and blending all my fears

it's tiredness on top of tired, these layers
are a quilted comfort that smother
my guilt in permanent pin-cushion anxiety

always feeling like a misfit, hiding
in the library where no bullies dared to tread
that's how books became my friends

words became my sword
and vocabulary my armour of self-defence
calling people things they couldn't comprehend

they had no idea how to respond
until the only answer became their fist
in response to my punchline

76

swearing in multiple syllables
rewarded by multiple bruises
but it also had other uses

word-play was my spur
reverberating throughout my life
have you swallowed a dictionary?

this memory reminds me to catch
my words in my breath
and put my voice away

until finding the safety
of the never-ending ripples
of the spoken word community

finally, a sun-dappled, leafy sanctuary
where I can always be seen and heard

I took the pen
(after Tony Walsh)

when I was young

people snubbed my geeky traits
because words became my friends

so many of them!

never-ending ways to say
I'm here for you

I retreated into poetry

but now my 2 passions combine
I write my love for people
in every line   be kind

My Blind Mind

A black hole
not yet mapped or photographed

It has space

Infinite space

        Unboundaried space

                to roam
roam
        voraciously

It plays with metaphor and meaning
It pounces on rhyme and feelings

Emotions flood this space
rain down my face
guttering into my pen

Words weep from the point
puddle on the page
drowning out your voice

making my mind –
that invisible, lonely bleakness –
      known

Worlds Apart

i write without the need to punctuate
my poetry breathes the lines
my mind creates
i don't stop unless
the world demands i rest
and then i rhythm my way
to the next stress

as i beat my fists
on tables – my painful chest –
and then i'm head banging
brick wall bleeding
in the same symphony
of misunderstanding

yes the world demands i rest
but that's a world which hears a different drum beat
and not the one that my feet follow
i dance a different path

my vision is unique – extra-terrestrial
my beliefs – other worldly – celestial

i am unbiased by my birth
my childhood and my conscious brain
my words are a persistent rain
and i want the world to be as skin soaked
as me, to feel the cold shoulder
of contempt and judgement
when what i meant has been twisted
by a selfish mind to be the negative
of my positive intent

and i'm headbanging
brick wall bleeding
in the same symphony
of perpetual misunderstanding

my vision is unique – extra-terrestrial
my beliefs – other worldly – celestial

we stand
holding our contempt
with no way to bridge
and this time
i will stand alone

on opposite sides
between us
this divide
i will not hide
my poetry in hand

my forehead blood spattered
as i pound the point
that – to me – matters

did you know not every brain
trips a logical path
that sometimes i can laugh
at pain and see a way to reconcile
impossible and unpopular
with unconditional love
to legitimise the needs of those we criminalise
because we do not know their world

and i'm head banging
brick wall bleeding
in the same symphony
of perpetual misunderstanding

my vision is unique – extra terrestrial
my beliefs – other worldly – celestial
the brick wall and me
we are interplanetary
irreconcilably different

and this space, this community
makes that difference we all yearn for

appreciation and unity

Haemorrhage

When sadness ravages my
sanity and nobody can
see or hear me

I bleed poetry

When you say I don't fit
or I'm not welcome
I reach for the pen

As the words drip
from the wounds
I simmer with rage

I bleed poetry

all over
the
page.

Who Am I?

'I can shake off everything as I write; my sorrows disappear, my courage is reborn' – Anne Frank

'Who am I,
in all this world of possibility, how can
I have been born?' I would shake
my head in disbelief. The odds are off:
1 in 400 trillion. Everything
else more worthy than me, as
I'm left wondering why was I
born at all. You rejected me, so I write

myself into the world through my
creativity. I gain agency over my sorrows.
My many melancholies disappear
and gradually I look forward to my
tomorrows, with inspired courage
growing from determination that this is
the only way to stake my claim and be reborn.

I have no clique

                I fit perfectly
then don't fit
                I belong
      where logic   and poetry   lie side by side

I'm the space

between verses

the perfect punctuation! and artificial alliteration?
I'm the bigger picture of scientific discipline
I'm the beginning,   the opportunity,
             the proof,
the indisputable evidence   that outliers succeed
      through   difference.

Chaos and creativity   collide in my persona.
      I am in-between
the wave   and the element,
both a part   and the whole,
the thought and the sentiment.

I am the horse that   bolted
and the stable gate.

The opportunity missed.
The opportunity taken.
The opportunity lying in wait.

Riddle Me This
(Ode to Dr. Seuss)

I'm the Kate in the Hat.
I love a good moral,
riddled and rhymed.
Across short,
hard-hitting,
alliterative
lines.

I was mischievous,
naughty, an imposter, an imp.
My attitude cheeky
like the Quail, Skritz and Skrink!

The morals you taught
helped me do what was right
until I reached puberty.
And then I rebelled:
Your stories and values
could all go to hell
or the local jumble sale!

I'd made it this far; I'd make it alone.

Then I got married,
had kids of my own.
I turned back to the stories
I heard you tell,

I wanted my children
to love you as well.
And I remembered
who I most related to.
We both had Trouble
getting into Solla Sollew!

But I was the Trouble
in many different forms,
and you showed me the way
to challenge these norms.

Now I'm older and wiser
and I've made my own path.
I look back at my Troubles
and just have to laugh;
I made them myself
by being the antagonist!

So now I'm claiming my place
as Plucky Protagonist!
And it's here where I'm happiest:

A hat wearing, verse sharing,
Heroic Maverick
in a variety-fuelled life;
now *that* is poetic!

Acknowledgements

To my Mum - without you I wouldn't have survived a difficult childhood and thrived with my awe, wonder and love still intact. I got my self-belief from you. To Carol, my sister, we shared so much.

To Shaun, James and Maria – you made our family whole: we all grew together. Happiness and poetry ensued from your beauty and truth.

To all the people that made me feel like I was broken you shall remain nameless, although your careless words and thoughtless voices helped shape who I didn't want to be. I learnt from you.

'Words create worlds' is the constructionist principle, and 'what we focus on grows' is the poetic principle, of Appreciative Inquiry (David Cooperrider). This strengths-based approach underpins my philosophy to life.

To the managers who helped me grow as a leader and made me feel like a person not a number or a problem to solve - Mel Moss, Pete Watson, Mike Pringle, Paul DeVivo, Steve Taylor, Marco Eijsackers and Rich Lovely.

To my poetry pals – Suzy Aspell, Phoenix Ruddock, Cathy Carson, Clive Oseman, Nick Lovell. You taught me how to embrace my poetic heart. You restored my faith in spoken word.

To Ashley Edge, my editor, mentor, co-host and friend - I honestly could not have done this without you. You showed me what true connection and authentic voice really is.

To G, your spontaneity and creativity are awesome, the design you crafted is picture perfect.

And to the very many poets who have been on this journey with me - Wendy Pratt, Leanne Moden, Rose Drew, Becky Who, Nathalie Sallegren, Jamie McCormick, Charlotte Faulconbridge. Each of you sharing your words and your truths have made me a better person.

To the Spoken Word Community as a whole - a heartfelt thanks, I am Un/Broken because of you.

Bio

Dr Kate Jenkinson is scientist and poet reconciled. She is one of a handful of LinkedIN Business Poets. She likes hats and writes about the many ones she wears. She is well known for wearing wonderfully diverse and colourful hats when she performs and remembered for making people cry - in a good way.

In 2022 she performed her TEDx talk Poetry Never Abandons Us. Kate is a sought-after Speaker and Spoken Word Artist appearing at TEDx events in the North-West and most recently TEDx Amsterdam Women, the Sheffield Coaching Exchange Conference and the opening keynote for the South Yorkshire Women's Institute. She incorporates her love of words and poetry into her business as well as using her creativity in her coaching.

As a commissioned spoken word artist she performed her work for The Wood Street Mission at their 150th anniversary celebration at Manchester Cathedral. She can often be found crafting 'pecha kucha' style keynotes where 'Poetry is Leadership', as well as spontaneous spoken word finales for Charity Award Ceremonies, Leadership Conferences and TEDx events. Her Spoken Word Finale is the most memorable way to summarise an event and leave participants on an emotional high.

She has competed regularly as a performance poet at Cheltenham Poetry Festival; was winner of the Manchester Literature Festival's Poetry Slam, Runner up at Your Place event #42 and Oooh Beehive. She is also an accomplished page poet; published in Covid and Poetry, Rainbow Poems, Good Dadhood, Eyeflash Magazine, Steel Jackdaw, Love in a Pandemic, Flight of the Dragonfly and Feral (their first Mother/Daughter poetry and art collaboration). Longlisted twice for Butchers Dog – her ambition is to make it in print next time!

Kate founded Next Step HR Ltd in 2018, to house her creative executive coaching during the day and her performance poetry by night. She recently realised she was neurodivergent, so this and her aphantasia is a feature of her work and play. She loves encouraging new voices and co-hosts Prickly Pear Open Mic - second Sunday of the Month – online. She is the founder of the groundbreaking Poetry in Business Conference, launched in 2024.

Wherever poetry, science and business intersect – you can find Kate, and her hats, there.

Links

Linktree: https://linktr.ee/katejenkinsonnhr

LinkedIn: www.linkedin.com/in/katejenkinsonnextstephr

Instagram: @k8Jenkinson

Facebook: https://www.facebook.com/kjenkinson1

Website: https://www.nextstephr.co.uk

BRANDING BY G

www.brandingbyg.com

POETIC EDGE

PUBLISHERS

We are an independent UK publisher, collaborating closely with our authors to produce quality collections that capture the spirit of the writer. Raising voices that are often stifled, we shine sunbeams on minorities, those disabled by society's lack of accessibility and acceptance. Working with authors globally, no physical, cultural or emotional distance is a barrier.

www.poeticedgepublishers.wordpress.com
www.facebook.com/poeticedgepublishers

.

Printed in Great Britain
by Amazon